learning to **loveDANCEmore**

a performance journal

volume 17 · ***conversation pieces*** · october 2021

conversation pieces

A Shedding conversation

More than a year ago, before anyone had a COVID vaccine in their arm in Salt Lake City, an incredible performance took place in a backyard on the west side of Salt Lake City. Dominica Greene (now a former Ririe-Woodbury dancer) and Courtney Mazeika (who you may know from SALT) created *A Shedding* — "a donation-based, socially-distanced, outdoor evening of live performance created by and for Black, LGBTQIA+, Artists of Color, and allies in the Salt Lake community." It took place behind Courtney's house in Salt Lake's Glendale neighborhood.

The gathering "offer[ed] up the space to mourn, address, discuss, and celebrate our experiences both individually and collectively, including offerings by local movement artists, a guided post-performance conversation, and a collection of resources for actionable steps towards supporting antiracist principles and BIPOC rights."

This performance and the conversations it started about race, queerness and art making in our current moment are important. (Disclosure: I had a bit part in Alex Barbier's *Sometimes Dance is Bullshit.*) Somehow *A Shedding* didn't get a review, but as loveDANCEmore editor, I didn't want *A Shedding* to go unremarked. So, in October 2020, I invited a couple attendees over to my backyard to continue the conversation.

What follows is a transcribed discussion between two brilliant artists who saw the evening: Gabby Huggins (then a teaching artist, now executive director of Art Access) and Daniel Do (an RDT dancer). The conversation has been edited for clarity and length. The photos below are by Tori Duhaime, who, along with jo Blake, moderated the talkbacks at Courtney's home.

– SBH, editor

loveDANCEmore: Can you start by telling us what brought you to see *A Shedding*?

Daniel Do: I came to *A Shedding* through Dominica [Greene]. She had been talking about wanting to bring dance to a nontraditional proscenium stage. We were actually in Courtney's backyard and we thought, "this place is beautiful, we should create a show here." It had to have been before coronavirus. We weren't wearing masks. *[Daniel was a volunteer for one of the two performances, mopping the stage down between acts.]*

Gabby Huggins: I came to *A Shedding* because a friend of mine, who is a dancer as well, sent me the RSVP. It was really wonderful to see the content of that work in that space, and in that neighborhood. It was a very meaningful place for me to be, personally, and the work just made that experience deeper.

A Shedding happened in Glendale and I grew up in Rose Park. It's weird to be in a place in my life where I want to be able to afford housing in that neighborhood. Given all the conversation about gentrification, it's interesting to be at a white person's house in Glendale. At the same time, a lot of the gentrifiers that I know are people who are young artists, who I think have some sort of awareness of their impact on that space. In that sense, it was cool to see white space relinquished to POC and queer performance.

Growing up here, I was really lucky to have a dance community at West High School, where Hilary Carrier taught. It was very clear when we would go to the annual UDEO conference: no company is like ours. We had a diverse company and even the kids who were white in our company were weird, white, queer kids. "Alt" children in this sea of white, Mormon, drill team and contemporary dancer companies. In general, I don't think that the arts community here in Salt Lake feels like a space for POC or queer people. That exclusionary nature made this event, which centered POC and queer bodies, feel really empowering and reflective.

Daniel: I actually grew up in Glendale, so, the venue was really close to my childhood home, though I don't really go to that area anymore. My family moved out to West Valley when I was in sixth grade. I also feel very lucky that I went to a really diverse high school and was on the dance company there and, yeah, you'd go to these conferences and see the stark differences between companies. And I feel that most of the people who were on my dance company either started dancing in high school or in junior high through the public education system and there were very few of us that actually went to a studio growing up. I feel very grateful to have found dance by taking it as an elective. It felt like home, being in that space. There's a lack of events like this happening in the Salt Lake community, and I had been blind to that.

Gabby: There's something unique about seeing other people of color dancing, even if I'm not going to become friends with them. It's important to find that they're real, especially here. It's sad to think that there is a community of POC, queers, dancers, artists here and that we're just not organized. We're not around each other. That's why I appreciated *A Shedding*. It was an intentional organizing of POC queer artists together. Existimos [a local activist organization] does this too — they take the different silos that we exist within and bring us together so that we can have a coalition of POC queer artists.

I think a lot of people watch dance and say to themselves, "What the fuck is this? I don't understand," because dance is often built to be exclusive. *A Shedding* was accessible to a broader swath of the community. It was a powerful evening, I started crying.

loveDANCEmore: Which piece made you cry?

Gabby: Dominica [Greene's piece *Fitting/Standing*] really fucked me up — the repetitive motions. It was about cooning and

Dominica Greene, photo by Tori Duhaime.

shucking and jiving. I felt it so deeply. It was so indicative of what the entire show is about and why we're all here watching this work. But also, as a Black person in this place, all the time, I feel like that's a performance. A really shitty fucked up performance that's exhausting.

Daniel: Trying to please the white man, essentially. Or thinking, "tell me that I'm worth it, or I'm just like you." Why am I trying so hard to be like you? I think it's reflective of growing up in a community that's so predominately white. You feel like you are the odd man out and instead of owning that, for me personally, I felt myself wanting to blend in and do whatever it took to fit in. I sensed that in Dom's solo. She was doing these moves, trying to execute them perfectly to get some kind of validation.

Gabby: Right, while the work and the moves themselves are reinforcing ideas about you as a POC inherently, anyway. You're doing these moves, you're shucking and jiving, it's reinforcing that you're different. It's very simple, but there's so much pain.

Daniel: Laja's piece really resonated with me as well because I see myself in her shoes, having that conversation and seeing how far that conversation can escalate was really interesting. Whenever I've been asked "where are you from, or, where are you *from* from?" I just politely answer and move on. But no — what if I actually challenge you and ask you why you're phrasing the question that way? Obviously, I know what you're trying to get at. I feel like now, I'm gonna make them work. If they want to know more, they have to tell me why they want to know more.

Gabby: I've known Laja for a long time. It was funny to realize that she is racially ambiguous to some people — to me Laja is white. It was interesting to watch someone that I know is white

Luja Field, photo by Tori Duhaime.

processing that "otherness." I've never thought of her having to deal with that question, "Where do I belong?"

Daniel: I'm one-hundred-percent Vietnamese and I fully lean into that identity. Entering the Salt Lake City queer scene has been an interesting journey. I meet a lot of biracial gay men who are totally leaning into their whiteness, to the point where I feel like they're trying to erase their "otherness." It's been an interesting world to navigate. I think Masio Sangster's piece, *F@@GT!*, touched on that a bit too. He pushed himself in his solo to talk about what being a queer man is like and what that journey has been like for him, and being fetishized. I just loved all of the queerness he was exploring — there was some drag in there. It felt very personal. I felt very honored to be able to witness him exploring his faggotry.

Gabby: I loved his piece. I thought it was a great way to come back from intermission. It made me think of a friend of mine. A very specific experience of gay maleness. Mase talked the whole time, so, it was almost a monologue. He very directly addressed race and queerness. It relates to what you talked about earlier, Daniel, your experience of being a gay man here, and watching other brown or biracial men not *be* brown because they're gay. He really addressed that. "Am I too brown, do they not like me?" It was very straightforward but super celebratory. It was a really lovely cap to the second half, in contrast to Mar [Undag]'s much quieter opening.

Daniel: I've known and loved Mar for a long time, and I was left feeling so proud. He's a beautiful singer and he rarely shares his voice with anyone. The fact that he sang a song in Tagalog was just, like, wow! He really inspires me because he's so proud to be filipino.

Gabby: It felt celebratory, but not in a showy way. A celebratory exploration of self, like I had a window into a part of this person – his ethnicity, his heritage – that seems really important to him. It was a nice opener, very grounding. It was also very sweet, very tender.

What about *Sometimes Dance is Bullshit* [choreographed by Alex Barbier]? I love the "sometimes." I love this piece. I just have so many questions, why the suit? [The dancers wore hunting costumes.] Louisiana [where Alex grew up]? The camouflage?

Daniel: I loved the fun that was made of classic dance moves. It still hits me, when [they] prepped for the pirouette and just did the clapping and the *fouettés* — that shit — it's so clear in my head. I almost fell out of my chair, you can just relate to that so hard.

Gabby: I guess I want to also put this piece in the context of the evening. I think it's so interesting that Alex chose to critique dance as an art form, as a queer POC person, the thing [she was] lampooning was the art form [she's] using. Dance is also everything. Amazing. Important. Beautiful. Fun. And so there are so many moments where — the grooving, again so funny to me — it's cutting, but hilarious…

Daniel: I've been talking to my therapist about this. Because we're starting to categorize what is essential. And I am wondering? Is dance essential? I've been grappling with that idea. My job was not seen as essential. I was on unemployment for sometime before I was able to go back with RDT. It just makes me question if it is this thing to be fun and explored, but also, there is a lot of importance and value people gain from dance. With every thing there are two sides, or more…

Gabby: Sometimes there are seventeen sides.

Daniel: It was refreshing to see the other side. Sometimes I think *wow,* I can't believe there are so many people right now who don't have a job and I do. It's me going in to dance and to rehearse something I don't even know if will get to perform.

I was impressed with the vulnerability that the younger artists in *A Shedding* decided to embark on. It made me reflect on myself and what I was creating at that age. It felt like there were a lot of things that Harlie [Heiserman] was trying to explore [in their work *excerpts from Tuesday*], and it reminded me of myself at that age — of wanting to say so much in my work. I felt the same about Mase's piece. I saw youthfulness.

Gabby: I found myself laughing out loud with them. They were laughing on stage, and my friends and I all started laughing too. Harlie's piece exemplifies the idea of *A Shedding* being a "showing" and not a performance, because you're right, they were exploring so many different aspects of their personality. [Harlie's] costume changes were really interesting. The movement felt like a morning routine. I was thinking about tropes and motifs: rinse and repeat. This routine of exploration, back and forth across the stage. It was expressive and intimate…

Then there was Courtney Mazeika's piece, *Not One Thing*.

Daniel: Her body is insane — what it can do. The physicality of her solo was what really resonated with me. I was like, "Ow. Why are you putting yourself through that?" In a way, it's similar to what Dom was exploring and putting herself through. I was just on the edge of my seat that whole solo. *Wow,* what are you going to do next?

Gabby: I would be so interested to know what people were thinking and feeling — how they would describe their own

Courtney Mazieka, photo by Tori Duhaime.

work. I think there's so much discomfort in Courtney's piece and then she kept going — why are you doing this? — oh, that looks so uncomfortable! There were points where it's clear she doesn't want to.

To me, it resonated as the constant process of making consolations. You're not doing it for yourself, you're doing it for someone else. I think you're really spot on, Daniel, in connecting it to Dominica's piece.

Daniel: That's interesting, because they're the curators, too. You point out the moments when you saw her discomfort. Maybe that's a commentary on the discomfort of the subjects that are being talked about right now. In a way, connecting to an earlier conversation we had — doing the work.

Gabby: The context of the show was about centering QTPOC people, however those things intersect. When I think about Courtney's piece specifically, the recognition of the conciliations — I think it's interesting that your bring up *doing the work.*

Dominica's piece made me cry, and it seems like Courtney's piece was sort of about the same sort of idea, but I didn't cry, because she's white? And, so, then I was thinking, but there *is* queerness here, and womanhood here, so there are points of access for me, and then still somehow it feels very localized to her experience. I'm glad that there's recognition there, that it can somehow cross-pollinate, but I do think you making the connection between those two pieces is interesting. It goes to show we see other people and see ourselves in other people. It's interesting that you're an openly queer person — queer in a way that I'm not — and yet we're both attaching it to her whiteness, maybe because we're both POC?

Maybe something I was thinking was, "this is about queerness." But even talking to you about it, that something that's still not quite a lynchpin for you.

Daniel: I was definitely thinking that and I'm glad you said it out loud.

Gabby: I also want to say, one thing I really appreciated about this showing was that it started with a queer POC person. And I appreciate the way it was laid out. There's a weird "Olympics" situation happening — and the context of George Floyd and COVID made it more relevant — but there's something about it being queer folks, then queer POC folks and then queer Black women, and then — and I don't think Ursula [Perry] identifies as a queer person, I don't know — but, the structure was interesting to me, the way people were centered and the things you were left with closer to the end. Ursula being last as a dark-skinned Black woman was super important and powerful to me.

Ursula's [work-in-progress, *to matter*] was, from my perspective, the most classical, it felt like something you could watch in an auditorium. I think the themes I took away were also straightforward — *striving, falling, gaining* — a lot of struggle present in her work.

I really do think watching a dark-skinned Black woman dancing in that way was a powerful way to end *A Shedding*. It goes back to what I said about the intention of the show.

The show felt like it was supposed to be about queer and POC people but it actually felt like a show about Black people to me. I just feel like the blackness in those pieces — something about the context of what's happening is related to blackness.

In some ways, maybe the queerness gets lost, across the board. Not that Ursula's experience has to reflect that. Her being the last piece was important to me though, and it sort of erases this queerness that was happening. Does that make sense at all, what I am trying to say?

It's not a critique, even, it's just an observation. But I think it's interesting, the choice to frame a showing in queer and POC contexts. But there weren't a lot of moments where blackness and queerness coalesced together. And that's not a problem. Alex [Barbier] is queer. Dominica [Greene] is a queer person.

The ending with Ursula did feel very powerful and important, but I also think that it leans the entire show — and maybe I'm wrong to view it cohesively — but it leaves me with a specific attention to a specific identity.

Daniel: I am curious if it's because of what's happening in the world. I wonder if *A Shedding* had happened after the Pulse shooting in Florida, how that would have framed the conversation and our viewing of *A Shedding*.

Having worked with Ursula, knowing her intimately, a lot of her recent work falls under an umbrella of healing — from trauma in the past. Hearing her talk about moments in the solo reflected the challenges she overcomes at work. I've seen her face that in the studio, and so it was fascinating for me to watch onstage.

A Shedding should happen again. Period.

Ursula Perry, whose work closed A Shedding.

An hour (or so) with Bijayini Satpathy

Last May I had the pleasure of sitting down over Zoom with Bijayini Satpathy, a dance artist from India, who had recently finished staging a new show, *Pranati, An Obeisance*, commisioned by Utah's Chitrakaavya Dance.

Satpathy has been called, "a performer of exquisite grace," by the *New Yorker*. She was a principal dancer and soloist with Nrityagram Dance Ensemble for over twenty years and has performed, taught, and choreographed all over the world.

Pranati was an incredible experience. It's certainly among my favorite viewing experiences of the last year or so.

Despite my lack of deep knowledge of Indian classical dance in general and Odissi in particular, there was much to appreciate — movement that marries abstraction, narrative and technical rigor; excellent music; and innovative ways of using the camera to simulate and even interrogate the vicissitudes of a live viewing experience. My conversation with Satpathy (which has been edited for clarity) only deepened my appreciation.

– SBH, editor

Bijayini Satpathy: I was in Utah in 2019 to present my solo performance, *Kalpana, the Realm of the Imagination*. Malavika Singh from Utah, who used to learn ballet at Ballet West, did a presentation and a master class for their company with me in August 2019. She joined *my* school in India in 2016, when I was teacher, principal dancer, and also director for training. She's been coming in summers and winters. In June 2020, she started training with me online.

Samuel Hanson: How does that work?

Bijayini: You know, even I was a little snobbish about learning from a medium that is not in-person, not having the teacher in front of you. But actually, in 2019, I was doing a workshop in

A still from Pranati, by Eshna Benegal.

Atlanta, Georgia, and in my class, I had this dancer. He came from the Bahamas, and, he — oh my God — he moved so beautifully. He said that had learned a little bit of Odissi before. So I asked who he learned from and he said, "I don't know who to call my teacher because it's mostly from YouTube... and then I realized he'd learned two forms — I went and looked him up and I found that he was dancing Bharatanatyam *and* Odissi. And both very distinctly — with their very specific elements. So, from that day I changed my mind. He was my turning point.

I find I teach very differently online. I don't teach on Zoom. That's of necessity because I live in the very rural outskirts of Bangalore where the internet is really poor. I can't hold a five minute Zoom conversation.

But a lot of students were interested in learning [during COVID] and so I thought very hard. Also, I had separated from the school I was working with for twenty-five years. I was practicing alone without community and eyes on me for the very first time and I was very nervous about what my body was doing. And then I found a way to look at myself. I was videoing myself constantly. From that came the idea, "oh, why don't I video myself doing the basics, everything, the conditioning, everything that is in the training?"

So, I took two months and just recorded my practice and then devised a method of planning lessons with excerpts from my own practice. Basically I sent a few videos to students as one lesson, along with a very detailed PDF supporting the learning. And then I let them learn — study and imitate digitally, cross checking with the PDF — and I've realized that it's actually a much better way of teaching. I feel like the students are very invested and they're investigating the movements and discovering for themselves the intricacies. In Zoom, I don't know how it works. I feel a limit to the quantity that can be learned in an hour — in the way I want, to explain all the details — it would take a lot of time. So, in this video transmission method, I find that if the student takes one week to ten days: investigates, learns, practices and then submits to me — I find a lot of learning has already taken place. Dance learning is embodied. What they learn from one class in this method they can never forget. They've put their mind, body, and practice into it before they submit, and so they remember it forever.

Sam: Wow, that's inspiring...

Bijayini: I enjoy it because it brings me as close to the experience as I get when I teach. I have been teaching very intensively for a long time — twenty five years — I've had residential students who dedicate their lives to learning our art form. So there is a way of teaching that I've been used to and this comes very close.

Sam: So you were never in Utah for this process at all?

Bijayini: No, absolutely not. The two dancers [Prithvi Nayak and Akshiti Roychowdhury, seen on page 21] who do the duets, they have trained some with me. But all three of their pieces [in *Pranati*] have been in lockdown time.

Sam: Yes, these are the two dancers in India. [The show was shot there as well as in Salt Lake City.]

Bijayini: Their training has been both online and in-person when for a little while last year when things were open. The commute is also difficult. They have to come a long way to me in the outskirts — fifty kilometers. But a lot of the training is online. Even for their final rehearsals, they were going to a studio in Bangalore city and sending videos to me every day.

Sam: That's amazing. So did you find that stressful?

Bijayini: Very stressful in a way. Stressful because I don't know this way of creating work. But at the same time it was a relief that this was going to be on a screen. I was seeing the medium we were going to be presenting it in. So, you know the editing process was in that dimension. Sometimes what we see on video doesn't work live and what you see in-person doesn't work for the screen. But because these rehearsal and development processes were on screen, I could say, "oh, this doesn't work for the screen." In my head, the pattern works there, and maybe when I am watching these two dancers in front of me it might work, but not on the screen. So that also helped. But, I've never worked without seeing the dancers in front of me. That was nerve-wracking for me.

Sam: Tell me about the music.

Bijayini: The music was composed fifty or sixty years ago. These are traditional pieces. When Odissi developed into becoming a classical dance about seventy years ago, the guru whose lineage I am, Guru Kelucharan Mahapatra, created a whole body of work. He created the music with the composer back then. But for this performance, I commissioned a group of musicians in

Malavika Singh performing in Utah.

Orissa and I went and recorded them there. Chitrakaavya's commission funded it.

Sam: So these are dances that you learned from your teacher, and you performed them…

Bijayini: Yes, when I was a child I learned them within maybe four or five years. Students learn them. I don't know how to give you a parallel in terms of say, ballet — maybe it's something like *Swan Lake*?

All dancers of this lineage learn these pieces as solo choreography. My students will teach it when they become teachers — it's just a way of understanding how technique is applied in choreography in various flavors. One is a devotional dance, an invocation. The solo that Malavika Singh did, kind of embodies this idea of sculptures coming together to create movement vocabulary. That was the process of reconstruction of Odissi dance seventy years ago. The third piece explores how dance is subservient to melody. The fourth explores how dance develops in storytelling. How do you bring technique together with movement and facial expressions? What does it do to the body when you try to tell stories that are dramatic and epic in scope?

Everyone learns these. In solo, they have a different flavor. When you bring them together in a duet — I have only gone so far as a duet with this choreography — it shifts. Also, when Mala does the solo, I have taken liberties to make the piece more interesting to the eye as a solo.

Sam: So, these dances had to be remembered from the sculptures, seventy or so years ago?

Bijayini: Yes, not all of them. Let me say this. The piece Mala presents is actually the embodied archive of the reconstruction and revival of Odissi dance. Odissi dance has existed, according to evidence we have in scriptures and cave paintings, for two thousand years in the land of Orissa, or extended Orissa at that time. It has been lost for many reasons, many times. You lose dance for fifty years and that means you lose the blood memory. There's no trace of what the movement was like. You have the reference of temple walls that date back to the first century AD. The temple walls are full of beautiful sculptures and reliefs — musicians, dancers and other figures in dancing postures and playing instruments.

And so the revival process was looking at these sculptural forms and embodying them and creating movement vocabulary —

stringing them together. Mala's solo is structured in a way that it shows that process of recovery. It becomes abstract. It's a form. It stands alone by itself. It has a pattern, a neuropathic way of moving. So that's how Odissi has developed, but only for seventy years, so its a very modern form — thought it has a lot of history — it's also a very new form.

I have done a lot of research cross-referencing the scriptures we have and the dance traditions that have existed in the land of Orissa and thinking, how can we expand the boundary? Because there is call for that. It's only existed for seventy years. We should take the liberty… the ways the neurons work in this, we start to move in this way and follow the patterns. So, I have expanded the basic vocabulary that way… Sometime she stops in a posture — a frieze — so you can see that.

Sam: I love the way the camera moved in that piece, having seen so much dance online this year, this was some of the best use of the camera I've seen…

Bijayini: Yes, this was my third recorded production. The first was created for Baryshnikov Arts Center early this year. By watching the post-production process — myself on the screen — I realized certain things I wanted to pay attention to. I guided what looks I wanted, what perspective I wished for, so the editing was to my taste.

I feel like for anything online, it takes a lot more work. The energy from live interaction is absent. So, what you put out there has to keep the audience's attention. I would sit at the editing table and I would get bored. But the editing has to be subservient to the melodic and kinetic transitions, otherwise it can very quickly become about showmanship of editing — it has to be logical. I supervised everything through the end. Eshna Benegal, who did the editing, is actually a student of mine. So she knows the form. Each take is edited through maybe six times over, with minute details.

Sam: Can you talk a little bit about the dissolves and double images? I was surprised by how well those functioned…

Bijayini: Yes, but in some places the cross-dissolves, the double images don't work… when I watch my work I feel detached from what I am doing… if I am not drawn to something, maybe it doesn't work. I am not trying to be hypercritical. I investigate why it's not holding my attention, why it's not working. Then I give up things I would be very attached to in a live performance, like, "where is the curve of the body best highlighted? Is it this angle or another?" Sometimes in the camera neither angle works. Sometimes I may want to go close to the face. I often say I only watch the eyes of the artists. I get glued to the face, even when I am watching, let's say, Martha Graham Company. I don't watch the body or the choreography — I am glued to somebody's face…

So, sometimes, I thought, okay, we can Zoom in on the eyes, like in the [show's final] narrative piece, but then often that doesn't work. I feel like the fingertips and the toes of the dancers have to be in the frame. If they're not in the frame, I'm not getting the whole picture of what the body's conveying… I am still learning. It's only my third production for online consumption, I hope that I don't have to create a whole lot more for the screen.

Sam: Well, the good thing about it is that you get to see stuff from all over the world…

Bijayini: Yes, I just watched this delightful, amazing work by Israel Galván — a phenomenal flamenco artist who has broken all the traditional norms of the form. Have you watched it?

Sam: No, I haven't…

Bijayini: Please watch, please watch it! Israel Galván's *Maestro de barra...* It's stunning.

Sam: What else have you been watching that you recommend?

Bijayini: Some people are really making dance films. Basically this performance is dance, recorded. But some people are saying — and I agree to an extent — that it just doesn't do it justice, recording it. So they instead are making films with dance. Some of the films by Aditi Mangaldas are very interesting if you want to watch her. She's premiering a work tonight called *Lost in the Forest*. I'd love to see how she does it. She's a Kathak dancer from India.

Mark Morris is using his dancers in their own homes — he says something very interesting, he says, "I can't separate the dancer from the background, which means, if somebody has a certain colored couch, or drapes, you know, I can see the door behind and sometimes I ask, what's behind that..." So, the way he uses those elements are also very interesting to me. I don't know whether I would do it, but it becomes much more filmmaking with dance than a dance video. It's a different concept, but I admire looking at it.

Sam: Yeah, I do too. I have one last question for you, I was wondering if you wanted to share some of the stories in these dances. For me, I guess, the last one was the most —

Bijayini: Dramatic!

Sam: Yes! There's one moment where one of the dancers stops on a dime and her foot is out after a very swift kick. She just stops there all of a sudden there and it's very striking.

Bijayini: Oh yes, that one is the fourth [and final piece in the show] — it could be a whole volume of stories. This one's about the ten incarnations of Lord Vishnu, his avatars. We believe Lord Vishnu is one of the holy trinity — there's a creator, a preserver and a destroyer. And Lord Vishnu is the preserver. How does he preserve? When things go awry, when they go out of balance, the balance between good and evil — at least in a simplistic way we see it that way — Vishnu the preserver comes to set the balance right.

It is believed that until today, Vishnu has taken ten incarnations and come to save the world ten times. The way I look at it, these reflect the evolution of life: the first incarnation is a fish, the second a tortoise, third is a wild boar, fourth is a dwarf, fifth is a half-lion half-man — that's the balanced image of the dancer you are talking about — then comes a sage, but he also turns into a slayer, and then comes a noble king. Then comes an agriculturist, then an enlightened soul — the buddha — and the last they say is yet to come, but it comes as a comet from the sky, on a white horse with double swords. Two swords in his hands and he destroys everything in his path.

And for each of these incarnations — why did Vishnu come as this form? — there is a story. For me, it's also a teaching about the way we have treated the environment... I mean, these are just stories, myths. Why did someone feel a need to say God is in the fish? Or that God is in the tortoise? Or the boar? And then God is in a dwarf, a strange looking figure. These stories are asking us to treat everyone with equal respect. That's my take.

So, in the case of *Meena* the fish — in that age, there is a demon — there's always a bad guy! The demon steals the *Vedas* — the holy books of knowledge. Knowledge is for everyone, it can't be taken away into the hands of evil… It's the same thing with these holy books, the *Vedas*, the secrets of how creation began.

This one demon, who becomes extremely powerful, steals the books and hides them in the depths of the oceans. And so when something is in the depth of the ocean, you have to become a creature of the ocean to vanquish it. So Vishnu becomes a huge whale, and kills the demon and restores the books of knowledge.

Similarly, in the second one with the tortoise — I won't tell you all the stories — it begins with the Gods and demons churning the oceans of life — it's about man's curiosity — we are still working to become immortal, and also finding our way to the moon and Mars, expanding ourselves to the whole universe. So here, the Gods and demons have a sense that if they churn the ocean, magical objects will come out of the ocean, one of which will be the nectar of immortality. So they use a huge snake as the churning rope — this is physical churning, not mechanical churning. Gods on one side, demons on the other, they use a mountain as the churning rod, and in the middle of the milky ocean, as they are churning, the mountain begins to sink into the depths of the earth. But for the process to complete, the churning must go on. So Vishnu comes as a giant tortoise and holds on his back shell the whole mountain, so that the work can be completed. They say the octagons on the tortoise shell are from the churning — that's the legend.

And then the one you noticed: half-man, half-lion. It's talking about religious equality. The father does not believe in a certain deity and the son worships that deity. It's akin to asking, "If my father is Muslim, can I worship Jesus?" Can that freedom and integration happen? That is still relevant today.

So, the father doesn't accept the son's deity and asks "who is this God you worship, where is he?" And the son replies, "My God lives everywhere." And so the father says, "Does he also live in this pillar, this inanimate pillar?" And he says, "yeah, of course, He lives everywhere." So the demon-father breaks open the

Bijayini Satpathy, photo by Mahesh Bhat.

pillar and out comes Vishnu as half-man, half-lion. The father — demon though he is — has obtained a boon that he can't be killed by bare hands or weapons, he can be killed neither indoors nor outdoors, by neither animal nor man, neither in the day nor at night. So Vishnu comes out at twilight, as half-man, half-lion, he holds the demon on his lap at the threshold — neither outside nor inside — and tears his stomach out with his nails — neither weapon nor bare hand. It is in this manner that he is destroyed.

Sam: Wow…

Bijayini: And in the dance, it's very quick, a minute or a half minute per story. So it's very important for the dancers to understand the context and how we're interpreting the stories... I find the relevance of these stories — they were simply told as Grandma stories to us — retelling these stories from our perspective is very, very important. The dancers need to understand them, everything they learn is technique — they have to practice for years to get comfortable, to be convincing. To emerge as this fierce being, this superhero, we don't know what this being might feel like with a half-lion human body — just to embody that. It goes on. It would be a long session if I told you all of these stories…

Sam: Well, I appreciate hearing them. In that last piece I almost felt like I was watching a song or a ballad, with choruses that repeated certain elements and verses that told different stories…

Bijayini: You're right, there is a chorus, it comes back to saying "Praise of Lord Vishnu..." and in rhythmic punctuation between the stories the dancers continue the theme of the prior story. So, if it was the half-man half lion, the dance that follows carries the resonance of that narrative... and then it transitions to the next incarnation and the next and the next…

Talking with Cat + Fish

In preparation for covering one of their recent shows, *Fragments*, writer Arin Lynn sat down with four of the artists who comprise Cat + Fish, a local group that has been major player in the dance scene here in Salt Lake since 2014. Arin spoke with Cat Kamrath (artistic director, choreographer), Daniel Do (assistant director, choreographer, and founding member), Mar Undag (choreographer and project co-director for *Fragments*) and Emma Sargent (company dancer since 2018). This conversation, conducted over email, has been edited for clarity.

— SBH, editor

Arin Lynn: What were your inspirations for the dances you just premiered?

Cat Kamrath: My work, *Gathering I*, looks at how we emerge from the pandemic (whatever that means now) with a newly embodied sense of self and how this knowing comes back into relationship with others. Phrase work was created based on *dancer + choreographer* descriptions of the *sense + stretch* of skin, what it means to *meet + match*, and *relationship to self, others, + environment*. Approaching this as a work-in-progress allowed for there to be more focus on exploration and coming back to our dancing bodies.

Daniel Do: In this piece, my dancers and I explored emotions and feelings that arose inside of the pandemic with various directives and improvisational tasks and scores.

Mar Undag: I was just so excited to be in a live process with other humans again. I had an idea of what I wanted to create but I wanted to keep a sense of play and have the artists approach the process like a study, so that it would feel ever evolving and ever changing regardless of whether we used any "set" things or not. I didn't want to ascribe meaning to any of the movement or phrases, but instead for each of us to have our own relationship and understanding of the material we created.

Arin: What is it like being back in the studio and navigating partnering after so long living in contactless or minimal contact dance?

Cat: I started teaching back in the studio in September 2020, but I hadn't created collaboratively since our last Cat + Fish project in 2019. Creating this work took more time than in the past. There was definitely a longer process need to create, a longer settling of the choreography in the body, and lots of workshopping of the partnering moments. I tried to prioritize conversation and listening in my process so my dancers could feel safe and supported as we created.

Emma Sargent: If I am being completely honest, I felt a lot of apprehension about returning to a physical partnering practice after more than a year of distanced-only dancing. There is an undeniable vulnerability in sharing our corporeal selves, in all of their messiness with others. My newfound nervousness was particularly frustrating because partnering has always been one of my favorite modes of dance making. I felt very valued and held by the company during the process of re-learning how to touch and be touched. There were many awkward moments – when I stumbled trying to lift someone; when I realized that I was tensing my body whenever someone entered my "bubble;" when I hesitated before placing a hand on a friend's shoulder… I am filled with gratitude for Cat and other members of the company who set an example of how to engage with touch thoughtfully by communicating clear boundaries.

Arin: *Fragments* was a works-in-progress showcase, how do you envision these dances evolving in the future?

Cat: Our hope is to bring these works back in 2022 after some more rehearsal time, editing, and creating. I think our dancers would also like to come back to their bodies a bit more and develop clarity in the movement and partnering more. In past Cat + Fish Dances performances, we have quickly created work and then moved on to the next. We are looking forward to spending more extended time investigating this work. I am currently feeling that *Gathering I* should be a quartet instead of a trio, so that is my next place of exploration. We have no confirmed timeline yet — hopefully coming soon! — but we do want to revisit these three works again and perhaps present some others.

We don't have our next project scheduled, but we will make sure to post about it as soon as we do. Audiences can find us on Facebook and Instagram at @catandfishdances. Our website will be going through a re-design so stay tuned for that big reveal.

Ishmael Houston-Jones talks to Ching-I Chang

Ching-I Chang and I originally met at the American Dance Festival in the early 2000s when Ching-I was an undergrad at Shenandoah University. After completing her BA at the University of Utah, she lived for a time in New York, later returning to Salt Lake City to receive an MFA, also from University of Utah. Recently she choreographed and performed *How Forests Dream*, an immersive dance at Fou Gallery in Brooklyn, New York, August 2021. We got together one recent afternoon to chat at The Chai Spot, a quiet, peaceful café in that blurry border between Manhattan's Chinatown and Little Italy.

— Ishmael Houston Jones

I, probably tactlessly, opened by asking her "what did you think of my improv class at ADF?"

Ching-I Chang: [after a pause] I'm not sure. I think it was an opening...

Ishmael Houston-Jones: What were you studying before that?

Ching-I: Dance. Dance all the way. All kinds, because in Taiwanese training you have to do everything – Chinese Dance, Ballet, Modern, Improv. Jazz and Hip Hop classes on the weekend on my own time.

IHJ: When did you come to New York the first time?

Ching-I: 2009.

IHJ: And what were you doing here?

Ching-I: Trying to find dance work like everyone else. [She laughs.]

IHJ: Did you? Who did you work with?

Ching-I: I was actually lucky because Gesel Mason was our choreographer for our senior piece at the U, so I just contacted her and said, "I'm here and I want to work with you." And I had a great time working with her. I can relate to her process because she emphasizes a lot of improvisation and social justice work. At that time, she was working on a piece called *Women, Sex and Desire: Sometimes You Feel Like a Ho; Sometimes You Don't* — that's the whole title. So she was like, "Why don't you come to DC and travel with the rest of the cast." Most of the cast was living in NYC and we'd go down to Washington on the weekends to have long rehearsals. Gesel's piece was my first professional job.

IHJ: I love Gesel. How did you make the decision to go back to Utah to get your MFA?

Ching-I: I was dancing very intensely in NYC, because, you know as an immigrant you have to work continuously to receive your Artist Visa (O-1), to build up your resume. So I was constantly dancing with anyone, sometimes dancing for free. So after five years, I was basically burned out, and intellectually I felt that I needed something more. I also wanted to start to teach and also my mom kept saying, "Why don't you get your MFA?" — you know Asian mothers, they're always thinking about your future. [She laughs.] So I said, yeah, why not?

IHJ: Let me back up a bit, how did you choose University of Utah to do you bachelor's?

Ching-I: I was there for my undergraduate for two years and I felt I wasn't getting anything from that time because I had

finished most of my physical training at my previous school, Shenandoah University. So at the U I was doing most of the academic requirements like math, English, etcetera, just trying to finish my undergraduate education, so I didn't feel like I was having that much physical learning there, but I appreciated what they were teaching. So after five years here, I thought maybe I should go back there and actually find out what that place and the people there can teach me.

IHJ: And were you happy with what happened?

Ching-I: Yes, [emphatically] wow, it was like... I felt as though I was at a place where I was mature in a different way and I could work with so many different things — I got to work with refugee populations, and I got to work with special needs individuals and see how dance can be used as a way to facilitate spaces and dialogue with different people. That was something that really resonated with me.

IHJ: And when you received your MFA, did immediately come back to NYC?

Ching-I: Actually I was in Virginia, teaching for a year at Virginia Commonwealth University, then I moved to Shanghai for two years before I moved back here in 2019.

IHJ: What prompted the decision to come back to NYC?

Ching-I: Hmm, decision? There's really no place like New York.

IHJ: I agree. [Both laugh.]

Ching-I: Yeah. And I feel really at home here. Salt Lake was great, but at so many times I felt lonely, culturally I felt lonely there. I love being alone, but that kind of loneliness...

IHJ: Do you mean like culturally, or personally, or...

Ching-I: Both. Some things there I could relate to, but most of the time I felt like I could not relate.

IHJ: And then you worked in *Then She Fell*?

Ching-I: No, *Sleep No More.*

IHJ: Sorry, I haven't seen either and I confuse them. [Embarrassed laughter.] How was that?

Ching-I: Great. I actually worked with them in 2011, I was one of the original cast. It was great to be there at the beginning, making the work, because the choreographer Maxine Doyle — she's there but basically she's not the one who gives you the movement, we are the ones who are creating the movement and she just says "more of this, more of that." She was more like a director. So basically the original performers helped create the movement material, which was great because I love creating dances, and working with the people. And the majority of the people were from Contact Improvisation so it was great to be at the beginning there.

IHJ: And you went on to be the rehearsal director for the Shanghai production two years ago? How was that, doing the same piece over there? Did the work translate to a different audience in a different culture?

Ching-I: *Interesting*. It was very interesting. Very different. Because in New York it is *Macbeth* and Rebecca's story and in Shanghai it's *Macbeth* and the Legend of the White Snake story. So it's more rooted in Chinese legend.

IHJ: Did people respond to it differently?

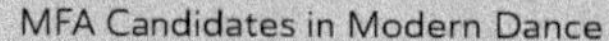

MFA Candidates in Modern Dance

GRADUATE CONCERT

works by:
Jessica Boone
Virginia Broyles
Austin Hardy

DEC. 2 at 5:30pm
DEC. 3 & 4 at 7:30pm

Free Admission
at the Marriott Center for Dance
and via livestream

more info: dance.utah.edu
photo by Todd Collins

Ching-I: Yes. The Chinese audiences are really concentrating when they watch performance. They want to follow you all the time, so in a way it's refreshing. Here in New York people are like — oh we can look at the set — they can and *do* make their own choices. Sometimes they just ignore the performers. But Chinese audiences are in your face, they want to watch you. Which is beautiful.

IHJ: So do you think working on this project affected your own work? The recent *How Forests Dream,* for example?

Ching-I: Definitely. But somehow I think how immersive theater was initially described was somehow degrading for *dance*. The majority of the public wanted to describe it as "immersive theater." But the majority of the work I have created is through dance. So I feel hesitant to call it immersive theater. Like the work in the sixties that was site-specific, that's essentially what we're doing — this immersive work — but the public completely commercializes it. When the producer, Echo He from *How Forests Dream* wanted to call it immersive theater, to draw more of an audience, I immediately told her, "Maybe you should put the word *dance* in the description." Call it "immersive dance." The team eventually surrendered to that idea.

IHJ: Good for you!

Ching-I: To be honest, I'm not a theater person, I'm not trained in that way. So I think we should give dance the credit.

IHJ: Thank you. Tell me more about *How Forests Dream.*

Ching-I: Echo He is the producer and also the set designer. It's a story based on her real life events. She was married for a couple of years and two years ago her husband passed away from a heart attack. It was so sudden, she didn't know what to do and she started her healing process. She started to dream. She had all these kinds of dreams and her husband was present in them, and when she woke up she would write these dreams down through poetry. A lot of the piece is created based on those dreams. And what's so special about this is we also went to his gravesite in New Jersey and through the intimacy of that, I really got to know Echo... She told me all the stories of what happened right after his death, all the details. And Ye Zi who is the director helped us conceptualize the whole event.

IHJ: So you were the choreographer, obviously. But how did Echo translate, or transmit the information to you?

Ching-I: Verbally. You know a lot of Chinese legend or folklore is passed along verbally. That's another thing I really related to, everyone was basically Mandarin-speaking, so there was something important about creating through mother tongue; it was so beautiful, there was no translation really, you heard the sound and somehow that transferred into your body. It was also energizing for me because this was the first production I was involved in that everyone was Asian. Often I am the only one in a predominantly White or Black cast.

IHJ: Wow. I really wish I had seen it. Was there actually language in the piece when it was performed?

Ching-I: Yes. So there is one point when an audience member is chosen to read one of the dream poems and I improvised in response to whatever I was hearing. So words are important.

IHJ: Was it in Mandarin or English?

Ching-I: It depended upon the audience member who was chosen to read.

IHJ: So what's next?

Ching-I: What's next? I'm really not sure. Because this year — we really don't know what's happening.

IHJ: It is so strange. Were you here in New York for the whole pandemic?

Ching-I: Yes. Basically they let go of everyone in Shanghai, whoever was from outside. So I came back here.

IHJ: It is such a strange time. You mentioned teaching before; do you want to teach again? Is that something you want to do?

Ching-I: I had that one year at VCU after getting my MFA and I thought, "Wow, I'm definitely not ready for this." I definitely feel I need more life experience, I need to have more of my own personal training and solitude in order to actually be in tune with what I am teaching. And I'm not a fighter, I don't like the dynamic of academia, I do not like it. I thought, I'm actually not doing my art right now. I'm just dealing with all this crap that I don't even care about. So after that one year I thought I should just give it a break. Teaching will always come when it's the right time.

IHJ: I actually enjoy teaching now, but it took me a long time to figure out how that figured into my art practice. I like it now, and I think it's important for me now, it feeds what I do artistically. But getting back to the time that we are all now living in. I have a project that is supposed to premier in San Francisco in November. I was just out there and we looked at the theater but we don't *know* if it will happen. Things change radically week-to-week. So we're wondering, if we can't be inside, will we be able to do something outdoors in San Francisco in November? It such a strange, strange time.

Ching-I: But there is also something really beautiful about this time too. Things are happening outdoors. I go twice weekly to Five-Rhythm practice with my partner. We just dance for an hour and a half outdoors with music. The practice of it — dancing with nature, dancing with people outdoors who are not necessarily dance artists, who just appreciate dance…

IHJ: I've seen a couple of things outside — Emily Wexler did a solo on the Hudson River pier at 70th Street and Eiko Otake did a memorial dance at the World Trade Center site on 9/11 at seven in the morning — that was very moving. But it's going to get cold here pretty soon.

Ching-I: [Laughs.] That's when I go home. I'm trying to find a balance between Taiwan and America.

IHJ: And I saw on Instagram that you got your US citizenship.

Ching-I: Yes, recently. So it's easier to travel back and forth.

IHJ: So, are you looking for more opportunities to present your work here? Are you working on anything new?

Ching-I: I have this principle that if I make work, I have to pay my dancers and now I can't. I don't have any funding, so financially right now I can't.

IHJ: That was the other thing I wanted to ask, because I'm mystified by people who come to New York now. I came here in 1980, and I worked lunch three days a week at a restaurant in SoHo and that was enough for me to pay my rent, take classes, and go to shows; and that can't happen now. I'm really baffled when my undergraduate students say that they are moving to NYC after graduation I ask them, how will they sustain themselves, their practice? How do *you* sustain yourself? You don't have to give me numbers… but I'm really curious.

Ching-I: You know, it's a city, so there are jobs. Mainly right now I'm babysitting. There's a huge awareness of culture, and I speak Mandarin, so a lot of parents are reaching out to me asking, "Can you talk to my baby in Mandarin?" Chinese-American or Biracial parents. I feel like I'd like to have children one day, but for now I get to play with kids and it also supports me financially. I've worked at a restaurant before so I know how tiring that can be. I don't feel that I need to take dance classes in New York; I do my own practice. I do my own Tai Chi, yoga, Bartenieff, improv, and ballet… We are in Jersey so we have space…

I feel that I'm not that young anymore, so I value my time. I do enough work so that I can dance. I cook my own food. I'm finding ways to balance all these things so that I can survive.

IHJ: Do you plan on being here for a while?

Ching-I: Yes, I think so. It's tricky though, not being back (in Taiwan) for a while. But I feel that you have to be here in New York for a while for things to happen. And these two years, 2019 through 2021, have been hard. Nothing is happening.

IHJ: Before I came to meet you I was at Movement Research for the launch of *their* new performance journal, and I saw ten or twelve people there who I used to see all the time at performances, you know, just to say hi or have a drink with afterwards.

I realized I hadn't seen any of them in two years. These people were a part of my community here. Speaking of community, I have my impression of Salt Lake, that it's not very diverse in a lot of ways…

Ching-I: It's hard, but they are trying, I think…

The University of Utah has outreach programs for refugee communities or special needs communities, so, for different programs we would go and volunteer…

Ching-I was a TA for Ashley Anderson's Dancers with Disabilities Classes at Tanner Dance, as well as for Pamela Geber Handman's Special Ed and Dance Course at the U. Much of the work she did with refugee populations happened through the Hartland Partnership Center and University Neighborhood Partners.

When I was teaching kids with visual impairments, I began to take the time to close my eyes to try to understand what that feels like. Even when I'm washing dishes or in an elevator.

IHJ: I teach a lot with eyes closed. Getting rid of the visual sense and heightening the others. But I think in the dance community especially, we are beginning to think about accessibility and a range of abilities dancers can possess. At Movement Research [where I serve as board chair] we've hired a person to check that all of our programs, studios, publications, etcetera are as accessible as possible. I think that ten years ago, we in the dance community were not thinking of this as much as we should've.

Where's your family? Do you have family here in the States?

Ching-I: No, they are all in Taiwan. It feels lonely sometimes. But all my friends are family here. And not just friends from the dance community, I have really good friends here. New York is pretty warm and open when it comes to finding community.

Contributor Biographies

Ching-I Chang has performed and taught internationally in major cities, in Taiwan, Canada, Ireland, China, and the United States. She has worked with many NYC artists such as Susan Marshall, Gesel Mason, Michel Kouakou, Maurice Fraga, Tiffany Mills, Bill Young, Kyle Abraham, Yung-Li Chen, Kiori Kawai, H.T. Chen, Phantom Limb Company and Loco 7. She was an original NYC cast member at Punchdrunk's Off-Broadway hit production, *Sleep No More NYC* as well as the rehearsal director of the *Sleep No More Shanghai* from 2017 to 2019. She received her MFA from the University of Utah School of Dance in 2017.

Trung "Daniel" Do was born and raised in Salt Lake City, Utah and received his BFA in Modern Dance from the University of Utah. He relocated to Portland, Oregon where he collaborated and performed with various project based companies before being offered a contract with Repertory Dance Theatre. He is now on his third season with the company and also serves as assistant director to project-based company, Cat + Fish Dances.

Samuel Hanson, a dancer from Salt Lake City, edits and directs loveDANCEmore.

Ishmael Houston-Jones is an award winning choreographer, author, performer, teacher, and curator. His improvised dance and text work has been performed in New York, across North America, Europe, Australia, and Latin America. Drawn to collaboration as a way to move beyond the known, Houston-Jones celebrates the political aspect of cooperation.

Gabriella Huggins, multi-media arts producer and former modern dancer, long worked as Community Programs Mentor at Spy Hop Productions. She's recently been named executive director at Art Access. A Salt Lake City native, Gabriella is working on issues of food justice, environmental racism, and trauma-informed therapy. Gabriella enjoys long naps, cold beers, and collaborating with young people in her community.

Cat Kamrath is a dance artist currently residing in Laramie, WY. As a dance performer, choreographer, filmmaker, and educator, her career has spanned the states of California, Utah, and now Wyoming. She received her MFA in Modern Dance from the University of Utah in 2016 and her BA in Dance with honors from Loyola Marymount University in 2013. Cat is a Certified Laban/Bartenieff Movement Analyst, studying with Integrated Movement Studies faculty Peggy Hackney, Janice Meaden, and Cadence Whittier.

Arin Lynn is a movement artist, multimedia artist, and hoosier based in Salt Lake City. They have recently had the pleasure of working with local organizations such as Finch Lane Flash Projects, 12 Minutes Max, and Queer Spectra Arts Festival. Outside of art, Arin enjoys fried food and collecting vinyls.

Emma Sargent is a freelance dancer, dance-maker, and performance artist living in Salt Lake City, Utah. Her creative interests include multidisciplinary performance, contact improvisation and partnering, and promoting marginalized voices through art. She recently completed a BFA in Modern Dance and a BA in Gender Studies from the University of Utah.

While at the University, Emma had the pleasure of working with choreographers and artists including Satu Hummasti, Daniel Clifton, Kris Grey and Maya Ciarrocchi, Katie Faulkner, and Daniel Charon. Recently, Emma has performed in multiple dance works by Dat Nguyen, and she is a member of project based companies Cat + Fish Dances and Deseret Experimental Opera Company. She has also presented work alongside LMN Mov't.

Hailed by the *New Yorker* as "a performer of exquisite grace and technique," **Bijayini Satpathy** was the principal dancer of the famed Nrityagram Dance Ensemble for twenty five years until 2018. In 2019, Bijayini decided to delve into a solo career as a performer and educator. Her recent US solo debut titled *Kalpana, The World of Imagination* was listed as one of the "Best Dances of 2019" in *Dance* Magazine. Acclaimed for her skill as an Odissi dancer and teacher, Bijayini is one of the most recognizable names in Indian dance today. She has performed alone, and with the Nrityagram Dance Ensemble, all over the world and has received many national and international recognitions.

Mar Undag started his dance training in Southern California where he performed and trained in various movement modalities and performed works by Malashock Dance Company and by choreographers such as Sadie Weinberg, Teresa Jankovic, and David Massey while attending Mira Costa College. He later continued his training at the University of Utah and performed in works by Juan Carlos-Claudio, Katie Faulkner, Eric Handman, Stephen Koester, and Stephen Petronio. During his undergraduate studies, Mar also created and presented his own creations in many platforms including the American College Dance Association, MiraCosta Theater, Marriott Center for Dance, the Jeanne Wagner Black Box Theater, Peery's Egyptian Theater, and Salt Palace Convention Center. He recently moved to New York City.

This publication received support from:

Photo Credits: *Cover image: Ching-I Chang, photo by Joey Wang. Inside cover: Bijayini Satpathy, photo by Mahesh Bhat. Page 8: Dominica Greene, photo by Tori Duhaime. Page 10: Laja Field, photo by Tori Duhaime. Page 14: Courtney Mazieka, photo by Tori Duhaime. Page 19: Ursula Perry, photo by Tori Duhaime. Page 21: A still from* Pranati, *in which we see lighting by Sujay Saple, photographed in Bangalore by Eshna Benegal. Page 24: Malavika Singh performing in Salt Lake City, videography and editing by Wonderstone Films. Page 32: Bijayini Satpathy herself in a photo by Mahesh Bhat. Page 36: courtesy of Cat + Fish. Page 39: Ching-I Chang, photo by Joey Wang. Page 48: Ching-I Chang, photo by Joey Wang.*

www.ingramcontent.com/pod-product-compliance
Ingram Content Group UK Ltd.
Pitfield, Milton Keynes, MK11 3LW, UK
UKHW020231250726
13967UKWH00001B/295

9 781458 315014